RAIN FOREST BABIES

SLOTH BABIES

by Genevieve Nilsen

TABLE OF CONTENTS

Words to Know............................2

Sloth Babies................................3

Let's Review!..............................16

Index..16

tadpole books

WORDS TO KNOW

baby

claws

eats

hangs

sleeps

tree

SLOTH BABIES

This is a baby sloth!

mom

It stays with mom.

They live in a tree.

It hangs.

claws

Claws help.

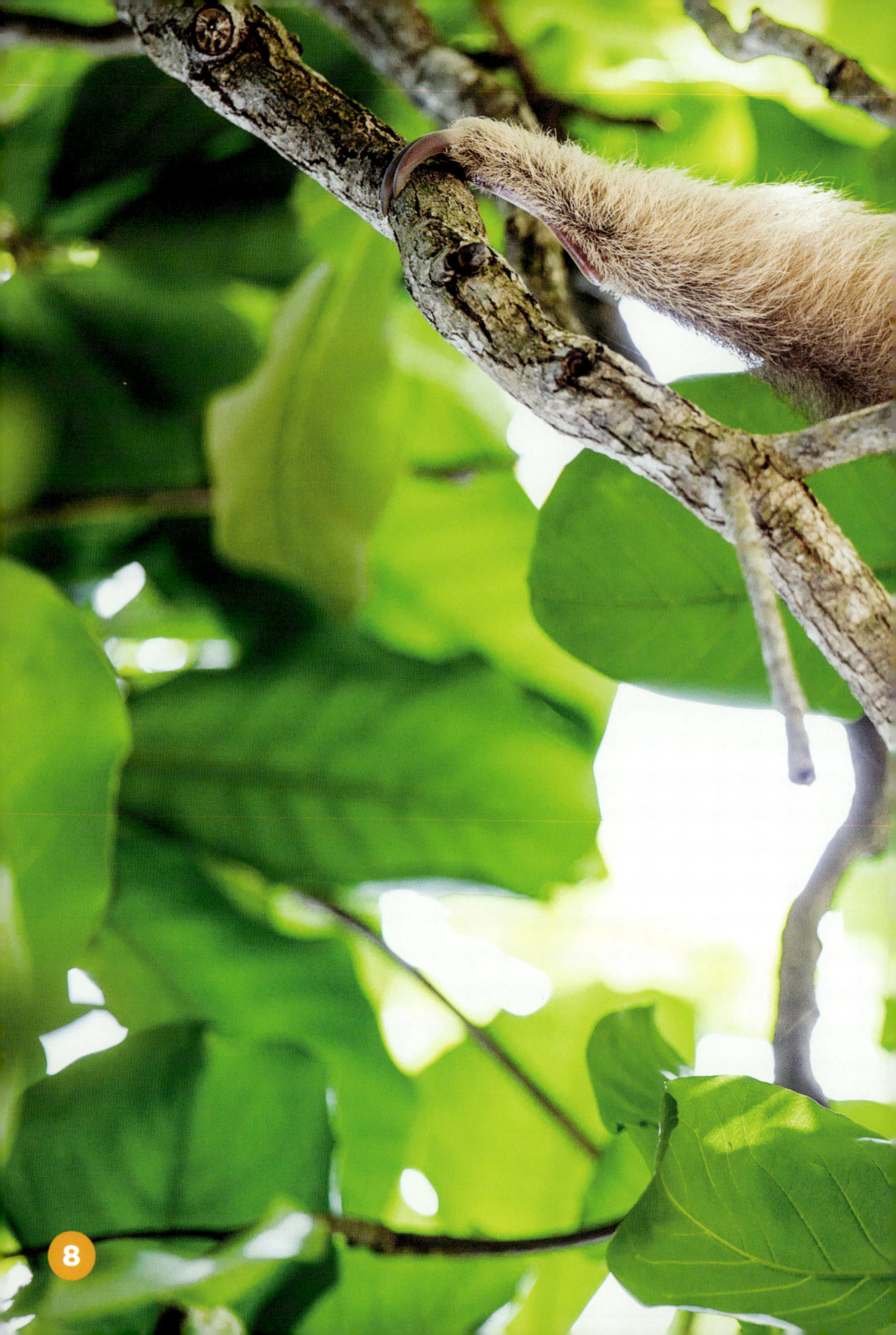

It moves slowly.

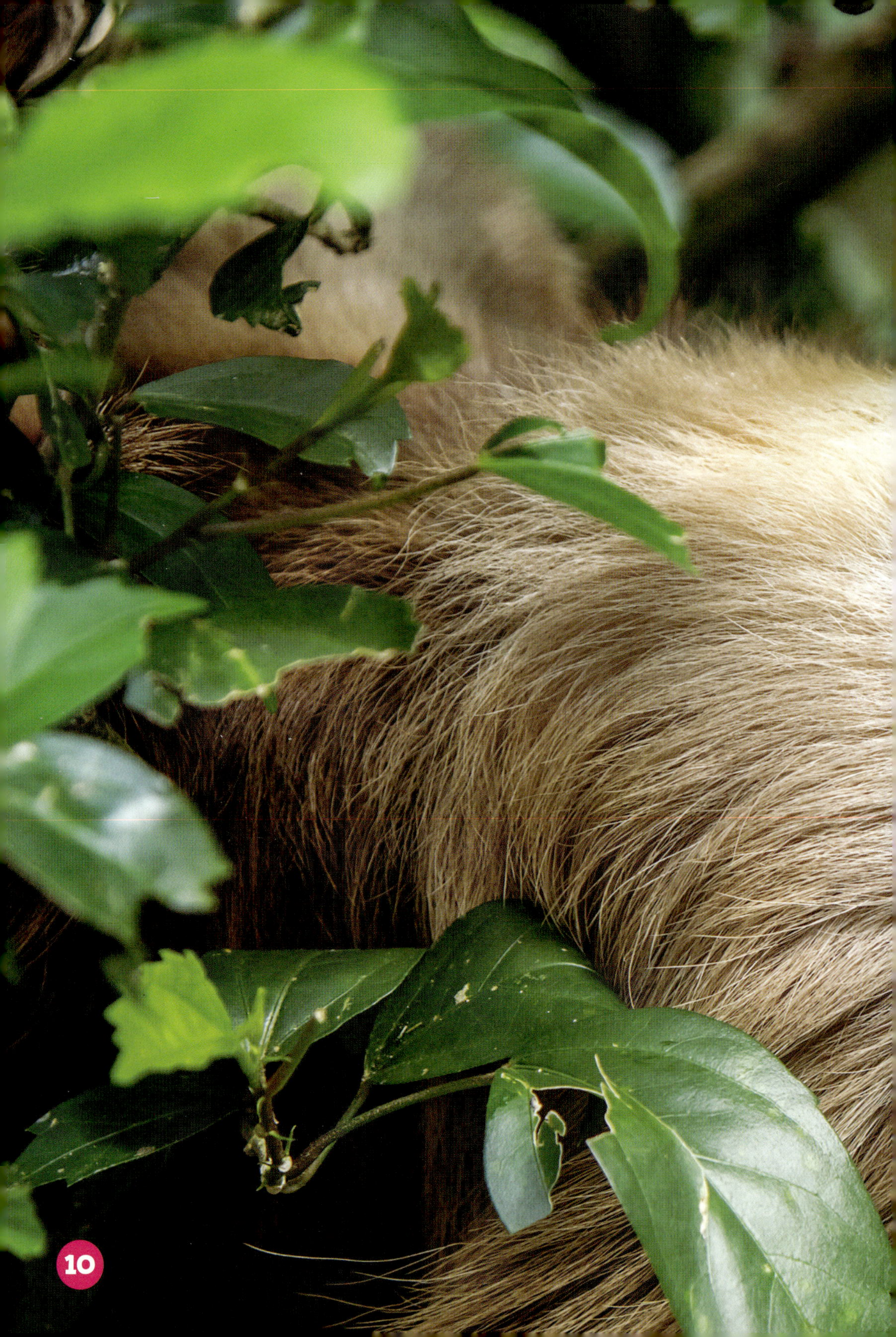

leaf

It eats.

It sleeps.